"Let the Monster Perish"

Henry Highland Garnet

Published Joseph M. Wilson, Philadelphia.

"LET THE MONSTER PERISH"

The Historic Address to

Congress of Henry Highland Garnet

HENRY HIGHLAND GARNET

© 2020 Westminster John Knox Press

First edition
Published by Westminster John Knox Press
Louisville, Kentucky

20 21 22 23 24 25 26 27 28 29—10 9 8 7 6 5 4 3 2 1

All rights reserved. No part of this book may be reproduced or transmitted in any form or by any means, electronic or mechanical, including photocopying, recording, or any information storage or retrieval system, without permission in writing from the publisher. For information, address Westminster John Knox Press, 100 Witherspoon Street, Louisville, Kentucky 40202-1396. Or contact us online at www.wjkbooks.com.

Book design by Erika Lundbom-Krift
Cover design by Allison Taylor
Cover art: Engraving of Henry Highland Garnet used courtesy of the Presbyterian Historical Society, Presbyterian Church (U.S.A.) (Philadelphia, PA).

Library of Congress Cataloging-in-Publication Data

Names: Garnet, Henry Highland, 1815-1882, author.
Title: "Let the monster perish" : the historic address to Congress of Henry Highland Garnet / Henry Highland Garnet.
Other titles: Let the monster perish | Historic address to Congress of Henry Highland Garnet
Description: First edition. | Louisville, Kentucky : Westminster John Knox Press, [2020] | "Publication of the address 'A Memorial Discourse,' which Garnet delivered to the U.S. Congress on February 12, 1865"--Publisher's note. | Includes bibliographical references. | Summary: "In 1865 Presbyterian pastor and abolitionist Henry Highland Garnet was the first African American to speak before the U.S. Congress. Garnet's speech, titled "Let the Monster Perish," celebrated the end of slavery and pleaded with humanity to never let it rise again. His address is reproduced here along with a time line of his life"-- Provided by publisher.
Identifiers: LCCN 2020016808 (print) | LCCN 2020016809 (ebook) | ISBN 9780664266295 (paperback) | ISBN 9781646980024 (ebook)
Subjects: LCSH: Slavery--United States--Speeches in Congress. | Slaves--Emancipation--United States.
Classification: LCC E453 .G2348 2020 (print) | LCC E453 (ebook) | DDC 973.7/114092 [B]--dc23
LC record available at https://lccn.loc.gov/2020016808
LC ebook record available at https://lccn.loc.gov/2020016809

Most Westminster John Knox Press books are available at special quantity discounts when purchased in bulk by corporations, organizations, and special-interest groups. For more information, please e-mail SpecialSales@wjkbooks.com.

CONTENTS

Publisher's Note   vii
Time Line of Rev. Henry
   Highland Garnet's Life   ix

"Let the Monster Perish"   1

PUBLISHER'S NOTE

The 223rd General Assembly of the Presbyterian Church (U.S.A.) in 2018 approved an overture to recognize the Rev. Henry Highland Garnet, an abolitionist, educator, and Presbyterian pastor who had escaped slavery as a child. The overture recognized Garnet's prophetic witness, encouraged Presbyterians to study his life and Presbyterian seminaries to include the study of Garnet's legacy in their curricula, and authorized this publication of the address "A Memorial Discourse," which Garnet delivered to the U.S. Congress on February 12, 1865, making him the first African American to address Congress. The address later came to be known as "Let the Monster Perish," based on a refrain from the sermon.

The overture concludes, "Having ordained Garnet, still a fugitive slave, as an elder and then a pastor in the Presbytery of Troy, the PC(USA) has a responsibility to history and to the Creator to witness his prophetic voice and to let his words speak not only for those in bondage but for the spirit of unity and moral righteousness displayed by the American people in 1865 with the passage of the 13th Amendment. Garnet tells us today that the tough issues can be addressed, that right can prevail and that justice only awaits our courage to speak as God would have us to do."

This publication includes the text of his speech, now in the public domain, as well as a time line of his life. Punctuation and spelling are reproduced as they were in the original publication.

TIME LINE OF REV. HENRY HIGHLAND GARNET'S LIFE

1815 Born on December 23 as an enslaved person in Chesterville, Kent County, Maryland.

1824 Escaped with his family to New York City.

1826–28 Attended the African Free School in New York City.

1828–31	Worked on ships as a cook and steward during several sea voyages to Cuba and along the U.S. coast.
1831	Began high school in New York City.
1835	Began religious studies at the Noyes Academy in Canaan, New Hampshire.
1836–40	Studied at the Oneida Institute in Whitesboro, New York, graduating in September 1840.
1841	Had one leg amputated below the knee due to a sports injury suffered two years earlier.
1841	Married fellow abolitionist Julia Ward Williams. They had three children together, only one of whom survived to adulthood: Mary Garnet Barboza.
1840–48	Served as the first pastor of Liberty Street Presbyterian Church in Troy, New York.

1843	Gave one of his most famous speeches, "An Address to the Slaves of the United States of America," at the National Negro Convention in Buffalo, New York. The central theme of the speech of encouraging slaves to rebel against their owners was opposed by Frederick Douglass and rejected by the Convention by a single vote.
1850–52	Lived in England from where he spoke widely against slavery in the United Kingdom and Europe.
1852	Began serving as a missionary in Jamaica.
1857–64	Served as a pastor at Shiloh Presbyterian Church in New York City (now St. James Presbyterian Church).
1863	During the three-day draft riots in New York City in July, a white mob sought to attack Garnet, but he and his family escaped.

1864–66	Served as pastor of Fifteenth Street Presbyterian Church in Washington, D.C.
1865	On February 12, Garnet became the first African American to give an address, "A Memorial Discourse (Let the Monster Perish)," in the U.S. House of Representatives.
1868–69	Served as president of Avery College in Pittsburgh, Pennsylvania. While there, helped organize what became Grace Memorial Presbyterian Church.
1869	Returned to Shiloh Presbyterian Church as pastor.
1872	Helped organize the Cuban Anti-Slavery Committee to fight slavery's continued existence in Spanish-ruled Cuba.
1879	After the death of his first wife, he married Sarah Smith Tompkins, a teacher, school principal, and suffragist.

1881 Appointed United States Minister and Counsel General to Liberia by President James Garfield.

1882 Died on February 13 of malaria in Liberia. Was buried in Palm Grove Cemetery in Monrovia, Liberia.

SOURCES

https://time.com/5124917/black-history-month-henry-highland-garnet/

https://www.pbs.org/wgbh/aia/part4/4p1537.html

https://www.blackpast.org/african-american-history/garnet-henry-highland-1815-1881/

https://www.biography.com/activist/henry-highland-garnet

https://www.nyhistory.org/web/africanfreeschool/bios/henry-highland-garnet.html

https://scholarworks.umass.edu/cgi/viewcontent.cgi?article=2389&context=dissertations_1

https://archive.org/details/memorialdiscourse00garn/page/16

https://www.pcusa.org/news/2019/5/16/honoring-rev-henry-highland-garnet-heritage-sunday/

https://phs-app-media.s3.amazonaws.com/s3fs-public/HenryHighlandGarnet_full_2019.pdf

https://babel.hathitrust.org/cgi/pt?id=pst.000008490155&view=1up&seq=271

"LET THE MONSTER PERISH"

On February 12, 1865, Rev. Henry Highland Garnet became the first African American to speak in the Capitol building in Washington, D.C. His sermon was delivered on that day, a Sunday, within days of Congress's adoption of the Thirteenth Amendment outlawing slavery. A number of representatives in the United States Congress thought the occasion merited a public religious service, and they extended the invitation to Garnet. His sermon was titled "A Memorial Discourse," but came to be know as "Let the Monster Perish."

"For they bind heavy burdens, and grievous to be borne, and lay them on men's shoulders, but they themselves will not move them with one of their fingers."

Matthew 23:4

IN THIS CHAPTER, OF WHICH MY TEXT IS A SENTENCE, the Lord Jesus addressed his disciples, and the multitude that hung spell-bound upon the words that fell from his lips. He admonished them to beware of the religion of the Scribes and Pharisees, which was distinguished for great professions, while it succeeded in urging them to do but a little, or nothing that accorded with the law of righteousness.

In theory they were right; but their practices were inconsistent and wrong. They were learned in the law of Moses, and in the traditions of their fathers, but the principles of righteousness failed to affect their hearts. They knew their duty, but did it not. The demands which they made upon others proved that they themselves knew what things men ought to do. In condemning others they pronounced themselves guilty. They demanded that others should be just, merciful, pure, peaceable, and righteous. But they were unjust, impure, unmerciful—they hated and wronged a portion of their fellowmen, and waged continual war against the government of God.

On other men's shoulders they bound heavy and grievous burdens of duties and obligations. The people groaned beneath the loads which were imposed upon them, and in bitterness of spirit cried out, and filled the land with lamentations. But, with their eyes closed, and their hearts hardened, they heeded not, neither did they care. They regarded it to be but little less than intolerable insult to be asked to bear a small portion of the burdens which they were swift to bind on the shoulders of their fellowmen. With loud voice, and proud and defiant mien, they said these burdens are for them, and not for us. Behold how patiently they bear them. Their shoulders are broad, and adapted to the condition to which we have doomed them. But as for us, it is irksome, even to adjust their burdens, though we see them stagger beneath them.

Such was their conduct in the Church and in the State. We have modern Scribes and Pharisees, who are faithful to their prototypes of ancient times.

With sincere respect and reverence for the instruction, and the warning given by our Lord, and in humble dependence upon him for his assistance, I shall speak this morning of the Scribes and Pharisees of our times who rule the State. In discharging this duty, I shall keep my eyes upon the picture which is painted so faithfully and life-like by the hand of the Saviour.

Allow me to describe them. They are intelligent and well-informed, and can never say, either before an earthly tribunal or at the bar of God, "*We knew not of ourselves what was right.*" They are acquainted with the principles of the law of nations. They are proficient in the knowledge of Constitutional law. They are teachers of common law, and frame and execute statute law. They acknowledge that there is a just and impartial God, and are not altogether unacquainted with the law of Christian love and kindness.

They claim for themselves the broadest freedom. Boastfully they tell us that they have received from the court of heaven the MAGNA CHARTA of human rights that was handed down through the clouds, and amid the lightnings of Sinai, and given again by the Son of God on the Mount of Beatitudes, while the glory of the Father shone around him. They tell us that from the Declaration of Independence and the Constitution they have obtained a guaranty of their political freedom, and from the Bible they derive their claim to all the blessings of religious liberty. With just pride they tell us that they are descended from the Pilgrims, who threw themselves upon the bosom of the treacherous sea, and braved storms and tempests, that they might find in a strange land, and among savages, free homes, where they might build their altars that should blaze with acceptable sacrifice unto God. Yes! they boast that their fathers heroically turned away from the precious light of Eastern civilization, and taking their lamps with oil in their vessels, joyfully went forth to illuminate this land, that then dwelt in the darkness of the valley of the shadow of death. With hearts strengthened by faith they spread out their standard to the winds of heaven, near Plymouth rock; and whether it was stiffened in the sleet and frosts of winter, or floated on the breeze of summer, it ever bore the motto, *"Freedom to worship God."*

But others, their fellow-men, equal before the Almighty and made by him of the same blood, and glowing with immortality, they doom to life-long servitude and chains. Yes, they stand in the most sacred places on earth, and beneath the gaze of the piercing eye of Jehovah, the universal Father of all men, and declare, *"that the best possible condition of the Negro is slavery."*[1]

> "Thus man devotes his brother and destroys;
> And more than all, and most to be deplored,
> As human nature's broadest, foulest blot,
> Chains him, and tasks him, and exacts his sweat
> With stripes, that Mercy with bleeding heart,
> Weeps to see inflicted on a beast."

In the name of the TRIUNE GOD I denounce the sentiment as unrighteous beyond measure, and the holy and the just of the whole earth say in regard to it, Anathema-maranatha.

---

1. Speech of Fernando Wood, of New York, in Congress, 1864.

What is slavery? Too well do I know what it is. I will present to you a bird's-eye view of it; and it shall be no fancy picture, but one that is sketched by painful experience. I was born among the cherished institutions of slavery. My earliest recollections of parents, friends, and the home of my childhood are clouded with its wrongs. The first sight that met my eyes was a Christian mother enslaved by professed Christians, but, thank God, now a saint in heaven. The first sounds that startled my ear, and sent a shudder through my soul, were the cracking of the whip, and the clanking of chains. These sad memories mar the beauties of my native shores, and darken all the slave-land, which, but for the reign of despotism, had been a paradise. But those shores are fairer now. The mists have left my native valleys, and the clouds have rolled away from the hills, and Maryland, the unhonored grave of my fathers, is now the free home of their liberated and happier children.

Let us view this demon, which the people have worshiped as a God. Come forth, thou grim monster, that thou mayest be critically examined! There he stands. Behold him, one and all. Its work is to chattleize man; to hold property in human beings. Great God! I would as soon attempt to enslave GABRIEL or MICHAEL as to enslave a man made in the image of God, and for whom Christ died. Slavery is snatching man from the high place to which he was lifted by the hand of God, and dragging him down to the level of the brute creation, where he is made to be the companion of the horse and the fellow of the ox.

It tears the crown of glory from his head, and as far as possible obliterates the image of God that is in him. Slavery preys upon man, and man only. A brute cannot be made a slave. Why? Because a brute has not reason, faith, nor an undying spirit, nor conscience. It does not look forward to the future with joy or fear, nor reflect upon the past with satisfaction or regret. But who in this vast assembly, who in all this broad land, will say that the poorest and most unhappy brother in chains and servitude has not every one of these high endowments? Who denies it? Is there one? If so, let him speak. There is not one; no, not one.

But slavery attempts to make a man a brute. It treats him as a beast. Its terrible work is not finished until the ruined victim of its lusts, and pride, and avarice, and hatred, is reduced so low that with tearful eyes and feeble voice he faintly cries, *"I am happy and contented—I love this condition."*

> "Proud Nimrod first the bloody chase began,
> A mighty hunter he; his prey was man."

The caged lion may cease to roar, and try no longer the strength of the bars of his prison, and lie with his head between his mighty paws and snuff the polluted air as though he heeded not. But is he contented? Does he not instinctively long for the freedom of the forest and the plain? Yes, he is a lion still. Our poor and forlorn brother whom thou hast labeled *"slave,"* is also a man. He may be unfortunate, weak, helpless, and despised, and hated, nevertheless he is a man. His God and thine has stamped on his forehead his title to his inalienable rights in characters that can be read by every intelligent being. Pitiless storms of outrage may have beaten upon his defenseless head, and he may have descended through ages of oppression, yet he is a man. God made him such, and his brother cannot unmake him. Woe, woe to him who attempts to commit the accursed crime.

Slavery commenced its dreadful work in kidnapping unoffending men in a foreign and distant land, and in piracy on the seas. The plunderers were not the followers of Mahomet, nor the devotees of Hindooism, nor benighted pagans, nor idolaters, but people called Christians, and thus the ruthless traders in the souls and bodies of men fastened upon Christianity a crime and stain at the sight of which it shudders and shrieks.

It is guilty of the most heinous iniquities ever perpetrated upon helpless women and innocent children. Go to the shores of the land of my forefathers, poor bleeding Africa, which, although she has been bereaved, and robbed for centuries, is nevertheless beloved by all her worthy descendants wherever dispersed. Behold a single scene that there meets your eyes. Turn not away either from shame, pity, nor indifference, but look and see the beginning of this cherished and petted institution. Behold a hundred youthful mothers seated on the ground, dropping their tears upon the hot sands, and filling the air with their lamentations.

Why do they weep? Ah, Lord God, thou knowest! Their babes have been torn from their bosoms and cast upon the plains to die of hunger, or to be devoured by hyenas or jackals. The little innocents would die on the "Middle Passage," or suffocate between the decks of the floating slave-pen, freighted and packed with unparalleled human woe, and the slavers in mercy have cast them out to perish on their native shores. Such is the beginning, and no less wicked is the end of that system which the Scribes and Pharisees in the Church and the State pronounce to be just, humane, benevolent and Christian. If such are the deeds of mercy wrought by angels, then tell me what works of iniquity there remain for devils to do?

This commerce in human beings has been carried on until three hundred thousand have been dragged from their native land in a single year. While this foreign trade has been pursued, who can calculate the enormities and extent of the domestic traffic which has flourished in every slave State, while the whole country has been open to the hunters of men.

It is the highly concentrated essence of all conceivable wickedness. Theft, robbery, pollution, unbridled passion, incest, cruelty, cold-blooded murder, blasphemy, and defiance of the laws of God. It teaches children to disregard parental authority. It tears down the marriage altar, and tramples its sacred ashes under its feet. It creates and nourishes polygamy. It feeds and pampers its hateful handmaid, prejudice.

It has divided our national councils. It has engendered deadly strife between brethren. It has wasted the treasure of the Commonwealth, and the lives of thousands of brave men, and driven troops of helpless women and children into yawning tombs. It has caused the bloodiest civil war recorded in the book of time. It has shorn this nation of its locks of strength that was rising as a young lion in the Western world. It has offered us as a sacrifice to the jealousy and cupidity of tyrants, despots, and adventurers of foreign countries. It has opened a door through which a usurper, a perjured, but a powerful prince, might stealthily enter and build an empire on the golden borders of our southwestern frontier, and which is but a stepping-stone to further and unlimited conquests on this continent. It has desolated the fairest portions of our land, "until the wolf long since driven back by the march of civilization returns after the lapse of a hundred years and howls amidst its ruins."

It seals up the Bible, and mutilates its sacred truths, and flies into the face of the Almighty, and impiously asks, "*Who art thou that I should obey thee?*" Such are the outlines of this fearful national sin; and yet the condition to which it reduces man, it is affirmed, is the best that can possibly be devised for him.

When inconsistencies similar in character, and no more glaring, passed beneath the eye of the Son of God, no wonder he broke forth in language of vehement denunciation. Ye Scribes, Pharisees, and hypocrites! Ye blind guides! Ye compass sea and land to make one proselyte, and when he is made ye make him twofold more the child of hell than yourselves. Ye are like unto whited sepulchres, which indeed appear beautiful without, but within are full of dead men's bones, and all uncleanness!

Let us here take up the golden rule, and adopt the self-application mode of reasoning to those who hold these erroneous views. Come, gird up thy loins and answer like a man, if thou canst. Is slavery, as it is seen in its origin, continuance, and end the best possible condition for thee? Oh, no! Wilt thou bear that burden on thy shoulders, which thou wouldst lay upon thy fellow-man? No. Wilt thou bear a part of it, or remove a little of its weight with one of thy fingers? The sharp and indignant answer is no, no! Then how, and when, and where, shall we apply to thee the golden rule, which says, "*Therefore all things that ye would that others should do to you, do ye even so unto them, for this is the law and the prophets.*"

Let us have the testimony of the wise and great of ancient and modern times:

"Sages who wrote and warriors who bled."

PLATO declared that "Slavery is a system of complete injustice."

SOCRATES wrote that "Slavery is a system of outrage and robbery."

Cyrus said, "To fight in order not to be a slave is noble."

If Cyrus had lived in our land a few years ago he would have been arrested for using incendiary language, and for inciting servile insurrection, and the royal fanatic would have been hanged on a gallows higher than Haman. But every man is fanatical when his soul is warmed by the generous fires of liberty. Is it then truly noble to fight in order not to be a slave? The Chief Magistrate of the nation, and our rulers, and all truly patriotic men think so; and so think legions of black men, who for a season were scorned and rejected, but who came quickly and cheerfully when they were at last invited, bearing a heavy burden of proscriptions upon their shoulders, and having faith in God, and in their generous fellow-countrymen, they went forth to fight a double battle. The foes of their country were before them, while the enemies of freedom and of their race surrounded them.

Augustine, Constantine, Ignatius, Polycarp, Maximus, and the most illustrious lights of the ancient church denounced the sin of slave-holding.

Thomas Jefferson said at a period of his life, when his judgment was matured, and his experience was ripe, "There is preparing, I hope, under the auspices of heaven, a way for a total emancipation."

The sainted Washington said, near the close of his mortal career, and when the light of eternity was beaming upon him, "It is among my first wishes to see some plan adopted by which slavery in this country shall be abolished by law. I know of but one way by which this can be done, and that is by legislative action, and so far as my vote can go, it shall not be wanting."

The other day, when the light of Liberty streamed through this marble pile, and the hearts of the noble band of patriotic statesmen leaped for joy, and this our national capital shook from foundation to dome with the shouts of a ransomed people, then methinks the spirits of Washington, Jefferson, the Jays, the Adamses, and Franklin, and Lafayette, and Giddings, and Lovejoy, and those of all the mighty, and glorious dead, remembered by history, because they were faithful to truth, justice, and liberty, were hovering over the august assembly. Though unseen by mortal eyes, doubtless they joined the angelic choir, and said, Amen.

Pope Leo X. testifies, "That not only does the Christian religion, but nature herself, cry out against a state of slavery."

Patrick Henry said, "We should transmit to posterity our abhorrence of slavery." So also thought the Thirty-Eighth Congress.

Lafayette proclaimed these words: "Slavery is a dark spot on the face of the nation." God be praised, that stain will soon be wiped out.

Jonathan Edwards declared "that to hold a man in slavery is to be every day guilty of robbery, or of man stealing."

Rev. Dr. William Ellery Channing, in a *Letter on the Annexation of Texas in 1837*, writes as follows:

"The evil of slavery speaks for itself. To state is to condemn the institution. The choice which every freeman makes of death for his child and for every thing he loves in preference to slavery, shows what it is. The single consideration that by slavery one human being is placed powerless and defenceless in the hands of another to be driven to whatever labor that other may impose, to suffer whatever punishment he may inflict, to live as his tool, the instrument of his pleasure, this is all that is needed to satisfy such as know the human heart and its unfitness for irresponsible power, that of all conditions slavery is the most hostile to the dignity, self-respect, improvement, rights, and happiness of human beings. . . . Every principle of our government and religion condemns slavery. The spirit of our age condemns it. The decree of the civilized world has gone out against it. . . . Is there an age in which a free and Christian people shall deliberately resolve to extend and perpetuate the evil? In so doing we cut ourselves off from the communion of nations; we sink below the civilization of our age; we invite the scorn, indignation, and abhorrence of the world."

MOSES, the greatest of all lawgivers and legislators, said, while his face was yet radiant with the light of Sinai: "Whoso stealeth a man, and selleth him, or if he be found in his hand, he shall surely be put to death." The destroying angel has gone forth through this land to execute the fearful penalties of God's broken law.

The Representatives of the nation have bowed with reverence to the Divine edict, and laid the axe at the root of the tree, and thus saved succeeding generations from the guilt of oppression, and from the wrath of God.

Statesmen, Jurists, and Philosophers, most renowned for learning, and most profound in every department of science and literature, have testified against slavery. While oratory has brought its costliest, golden treasures, and laid them on the altar of God and of freedom, it has aimed its fiercest lightning and loudest thunder at the strongholds of tyranny, injustice, and despotism.

From the days of Balak to those of Isaiah and Jeremiah, up to the times of Paul, and through every age of the Christian Church, the sons of thunder have denounced the abominable thing. The heroes who stood in the shining ranks of the hosts of the friends of human progress, from Cicero to Chatham, and Burke, Sharp, Wilberforce, and Thomas Clarkson, and Curran, assaulted the citadel of despotism. The orators and statesmen of our own land, whether they belong to the past, or to the present age, will live and shine in the annals of history, in proportion as they have dedicated their genius and talents to the defence of Justice and man's God-given rights.

All the poets who live in sacred and profane history have charmed the world with their most enchanting strains, when they have tuned their lyres to the praise of Liberty. When the Muses can no longer decorate her altars with their garlands, then they hang their harps upon the willows and weep.

From Moses to Terrence and Homer, from thence to Milton and Cowper, Thomson and Thomas Campbell, and on to the days of our own bards, our Bryants, Longfellows, Whittiers, Morrises, and Bokers, all have presented their best gifts to the interests and rights of man.

Every good principle, and every great and noble power, have been made the subjects of the inspired verse, and the songs of poets. But who of them has attempted to immortalize slavery? You will search in vain the annals of the world to find an instance. Should any attempt the sacrilegious work, his genius would fall to the earth as if smitten by the lightning of heaven. Should he lift his hand to write a line in its praise, or defence, the ink would freeze on the point of his pen.

Could we array in one line, representatives of all the families of men, beginning with those lowest in the scale of being, and should we put to them the question, Is it right and desirable that you should be reduced to the condition of slaves, to be registered with chattels, to have your persons, and your lives, and the products of your labor, subjected to the will and the interests of others? Is it right and just that the persons of your wives and children should be at the disposal of others, and be yielded to them for the purpose of pampering their lusts and greed of gain? Is it right to lay heavy burdens on other men's shoulders which you would not remove with one of your fingers? From the rude savage and barbarian the negative response would come, increasing in power and significance as it rolled up the line. And when those should reply, whose minds and hearts are illuminated with the highest civilization and with the spirit of Christianity, the answer deep-toned and prolonged would thunder forth, no, no!

With all the moral attributes of God on our side, cheered as we are by the voices of universal human nature,—in view of the best interests of the present and future generations—animated with the noble desire to furnish the nations of the earth with a worthy example, let the verdict of death which has been brought in against slavery by the THIRTY-EIGHTH CONGRESS, be affirmed and executed by the people. Let the gigantic monster perish. Yes, perish now, and perish forever!

> "Down let the shrine of Moloch sink,
>   And leave no traces where it stood;
> No longer let its idol drink,
>   His daily cup of human blood.
> But rear another altar there,
>   To truth, and love, and mercy given,
> And freedom's gift and freedom's prayer,
>   Shall call an answer down from heaven."

It is often asked when and where will the demands of the reformers of this and coming ages end? It is a fair question, and I will answer.

When all unjust and heavy burdens shall be removed from every man in the land. When all invidious and proscriptive distinctions shall be blotted out from our laws, whether they be constitutional, statute, or municipal laws. When emancipation shall be followed by enfranchisement, and all men holding allegiance to the government shall enjoy every right of American citizenship. When our brave and gallant soldiers shall have justice done unto them. When the men who endure the sufferings and perils of the battle-field in the defence of their country, and in order to keep our rulers in their places, shall enjoy the well-earned privilege of voting for them. When in the army and navy, and in every legitimate and honorable occupation, promotion shall smile upon merit without the slightest regard to the complexion of a man's face. When there shall be no more class-legislation, and no more trouble concerning the black man and his rights, than there is in regard to other American citizens. When, in every respect, he shall be equal before the law, and shall be left to make his own way in the social walks of life.

We ask, and only ask, that when our poor frail barks are launched on life's ocean—

> "Bound on a voyage of awful length
> And dangers little known,"

that, in common with others, we may be furnished with rudder, helm, and sails, and charts, and compass. Give us good pilots to conduct us to the open seas; lift no false lights along the dangerous coasts, and if it shall please God to send us propitious winds, or fearful gales, we shall survive or perish as our energies or neglect shall determine. We ask no special favors, but we plead for justice. While we scorn unmanly dependence; in the name of God, the universal Father, we demand the right to live, and labor, and enjoy the fruits of our toil. The good work which God has assigned for the ages to come, will be finished, when our national literature shall be so purified as to reflect a faithful and a just light upon the character and social habits of our race, and the brush, and pencil, and chisel, and Lyre of Art, shall refuse to lend their aid to scoff at the afflictions of the poor, or to caricature, or ridicule a long-suffering people. When caste and prejudice in Christian churches shall be utterly destroyed, and shall be regarded as totally unworthy of Christians, and at variance with the principles of the gospel. When the blessings of the Christian religion, and of sound, religious education, shall be freely offered to all, then, and not till then, shall the effectual labors of God's people and God's instruments cease.

If slavery has been destroyed merely from *necessity*, let every class be enfranchised at the dictation of *justice*. Then we shall have a Constitution that shall be reverenced by all: rulers who shall be honored, and revered, and a Union that shall be sincerely loved by a brave and patriotic people, and which can never be severed.

Great sacrifices have been made by the people; yet, greater still are demanded ere atonement can be made for our national sins. Eternal justice holds heavy mortgages against us, and will require the payment of the last farthing. We have involved ourselves in the sin of unrighteous gain, stimulated by luxury, and pride, and the love of power and oppression; and prosperity and peace can be purchased only by blood, and with tears of repentance. We have paid some of the fearful installments, but there are other heavy obligations to be met.

The great day of the nation's judgment has come, and who shall be able to stand? Even we, whose ancestors have suffered the afflictions which are inseparable from a condition of slavery, for the period of two centuries and a half, now pity our land and weep with those who weep.

Upon the total and complete destruction of this accursed sin depends the safety and perpetuity of our Republic and its excellent institutions.

Let slavery die. It has had a long and fair trial. God himself has pleaded against it. The enlightened nations of the earth have condemned it. Its death warrant is signed by God and man. Do not commute its sentence. Give it no respite, but let it be ignominiously executed.

Honorable Senators and Representatives! illustrious rulers of this great nation! I cannot refrain this day from invoking upon you, in God's name, the blessings of millions who were ready to perish, but to whom a new and better life has been opened by your humanity, justice, and patriotism. You have said, "Let the Constitution of the country be so amended that slavery and involuntary servitude shall no longer exist in the United States, except in punishment for crime." Surely, an act so sublime could not escape Divine notice; and doubtless the deed has been recorded in the archives of heaven. Volumes may be appropriated to your praise and renown in the history of the world. Genius and art may perpetuate the glorious act on canvass and in marble, but certain and more lasting monuments in commemoration of your decision are already erected in the hearts and memories of a grateful people.

The nation has begun its exodus from worse than Egyptian bondage; and I beseech you that you say to the people, "*that they go forward.*" With the assurance of God's favor in all things done in obedience to his righteous will, and guided by day and by night by the pillars of cloud and fire, let us not pause until we have reached the other and safe side of the stormy and crimson sea. Let freemen and patriots mete out complete and equal justice to all men, and thus prove to mankind the superiority of our Democratic, Republican Government.

Favored men, and honored of God as his instruments, speedily finish the work which he has given you to do. *Emancipate, Enfranchise,*

Educate, and give the blessings of the gospel to every American citizen.

> "Hear ye not how, from all high points of Time,—
>   From peak to peak adown the mighty chain
> That links the ages—echoing sublime
>   A Voice Almighty—leaps one grand refrain.
>   Wakening the generations with a shout,
>   And trumpet—call of thunder—Come ye out!
>
> "Out from old forms and dead idolatries;
>   From fading myths and superstitious dreams:
> From Pharisaic rituals and lies,
>   And all the bondage of the life that seems!
> Out—on the pilgrim path, of heroes trod,
> Over earth's wastes, to reach forth after God!
>
> "The Lord hath bowed his heaven, and come down!
>   Now, in this latter century of time,
> Once more his tent is pitched on Sinai's crown!
>   Once more in clouds must Faith to meet him climb!
> Once more his thunder crashes on our doubt
> And fear and sin—'My people! come ye out!'
>
> "From false ambitions and base luxuries;
>   From puny aims and indolent self-ends;

From cant of faith, and shams of liberties,
   And mist of ill that Truth's pure day-beam bends:
Out, from all darkness of the Egypt-land,
Into my sun-blaze on the desert sand!

* * *

"Show us our Aaron, with his rod in flower!
   Our Miriam, with her timbrel-soul in tune!
And call some Joshua, in the Spirit's power,
   To poise our sun of strength at point of noon!
God of our fathers! over sand and sea,
Still keep our struggling footsteps close to thee!"[2]

Then before us a path of prosperity will open, and upon us will descend the mercies and favors of God. Then shall the people of other countries, who are standing tip-toe on the shores of every ocean, earnestly looking to see the end of this amazing conflict, behold a Republic that is sufficiently strong to outlive the ruin and desolations of civil war, having the magnanimity to do justice to the poorest and weakest of her citizens. Thus shall we

---

2. *Atlantic Monthly*, 1862.

give to the world the form of a model Republic, founded on the principles of justice, and humanity, and Christianity, in which the burdens of war and the blessings of peace are equally borne and enjoyed by all.

THE END.

www.ingramcontent.com/pod-product-compliance
Lightning Source LLC
Chambersburg PA
CBHW020857020526
44107CB00076B/2073